Annual Report on Vital Signs Monitoring of Wolf (*Canis lupus*) Distribution and Abundance in Yukon-Charley Rivers National Preserve, Central Alaska Network

2010 Report

Natural Resource Technical Report NPS/CAKN/NRTR—2010/468

John Burch
National Park Service
Yukon-Charley Rivers National Preserve
4175 Geist Road
Fairbanks, AK 99709
John_Burch@NPS.GOV

June 2011

U.S. Department of the Interior
National Park Service
Natural Resource Stewardship and Science
Fort Collins, Colorado

The National Park Service, Natural Resource Stewardship and Science office in Fort Collins, Colorado publishes a range of reports that address natural resource topics of interest and applicability to a broad audience in the National Park Service and others in natural resource management, including scientists, conservation and environmental constituencies, and the public.

The Natural Resource Technical Report Series is used to disseminate results of scientific studies in the physical, biological, and social sciences for both the advancement of science and the achievement of the National Park Service mission. The series provides contributors with a forum for displaying comprehensive data that are often deleted from journals because of page limitations.

All manuscripts in the series receive the appropriate level of peer review to ensure that the information is scientifically credible, technically accurate, appropriately written for the intended audience, and designed and published in a professional manner.

This report received informal peer review by subject-matter experts who were not directly involved in the collection, analysis, or reporting of the data. Data in this report were collected and analyzed using methods based on established, peer-reviewed protocols and were analyzed and interpreted within the guidelines of the protocols.

Views, statements, findings, conclusions, recommendations, and data in this report do not necessarily reflect views and policies of the National Park Service, U.S. Department of the Interior. Mention of trade names or commercial products does not constitute endorsement or recommendation for use by the U.S. Government.

This report is available from The National Park Service, Central Alaska Network website (http://science.nature.nps.gov/im/units/cakn/) and the Natural Resource Publications Management website (http://www.nature.nps.gov/publications/nrpm/).

Please cite this publication as:

NPS 191/108108, June 2011

Contents

Figures

Figures (continued)

Tables

Executive Summary

- Wolf populations have been monitored in Yukon-Charley Rivers National Preserve (YUCH) from March 1993 to present. Beginning October 2005 the project was incorporated into CAKN Vital signs monitoring program.

- Wolves throughout the greater Yukon-Charley Rivers area are targeted for monitoring of abundance and distribution. This past winter, wolf captures were conducted in December 2009 and February 2010. Monitoring radiocollared packs via radio telemetry flights will occur throughout the year with a concentrated period of flights each year in March – April and again in September – October. All field work is conducted using 1 or 2 biologists and 1 - 3 pilots.

- In winter 09-10, nine more wolves in 7 packs were captured and collared. Two packs were found by snowtracking. At least 2 areas where packs once lived remain without collared wolves and we hope to find and capture wolves from these packs in winter 10-11.

- A new measure was developed this year to help make management decisions quickly: the drop in counts of wolves from fall (September/October) to Spring (march and April). This year the counts dropped from 52 to 31 wolves, a decline of 41% which is outside the range of 14 previous years of data.

- The Fall 2009 wolf density (3.52 wolves/1000 km^2) was below the average of 4.18 for fall wolf density measured in Yuch since 1993, this was followed by a spring 2010 density of 2.10 wolves/1000 km^2 which is also below the overall average of 2.75.

- Fall 2009 mean pack size was 5.8 wolves/ pack.

- Fall 2009 average litter size was 2.8 pups/ pack.

- Only 1wolf was trapped or snared within YUCH in winter 2009-10 that we know of, from ADF&G sealing records.

- No substantial changes in protocol are anticipated for the upcoming field season for biological year 10-11 (May 1, 2010 – April 30, 2011).

Key Words

Yukon-Charley Rivers National Preserve, wolves, *Canis lupus*, radiotelemetry, population dynamics, density estimation.

Acknowledgments

This study was funded by U.S. National Park Service Central Alaska Network and Yukon-Charley Rivers National Preserve, Alaska. The skilled and safe aircraft support provided during the study by S. Hamilton, D. Miller, R. Swisher, and T. Cambier is always much appreciated. None of the work gets done without the pilots, they are there for every observation and capture, and are often the unsung heroes of most wildlife survey work throughout Alaska. Tom Meier and Maggie MacCluskie reviewed the report and made several helpful comments.

Introduction

CAKN has adopted a holistic view of network ecosystems and will track the major physical drivers of ecosystem change and responses of the two major components of the biota, plants and animals. Thus, CAKN has identified Fauna Distribution and Abundance as one of its top three vital signs. In general, CAKN wants to know where fauna are distributed across the landscape and to track changes in both their distribution and abundance. The Fauna Distribution and Abundance vital sign includes monitoring efforts for a suite of vertebrate species spanning the significant elevation gradient found in CAKN parks, and also including species of specific interest within each park. Wolves (*Canis lupus*), occur in all three network parks and are one of six keystone large mammal species in interior Alaska. Wolves are of great importance to people from both consumptive and non-consumptive viewpoints, and to the ecosystem as a whole. From a monitoring standpoint, wolves are considered to be good indicators of long-term habitat change within park ecosystems because they depend on healthy populations of large ungulate prey, which in turn respond to vegetation, weather and other habitat patterns across the entire landscape (Mech and Peterson 2003, Fuller et al. 2003). As a top predator, wolves can play a key role in influencing ungulate populations, and as a result may influence vegetation patterns (Miller et al. 2001, Ripple and Beschta 2003). The effects of wolves on ungulate populations may be important determinants of ungulate availability for subsistence harvest on NPS Park and Preserve lands in Alaska, and harvest by the general public on NPS Preserve lands (National Park Service 2001).

Wolves are a species specifically identified in the enabling legislation and management objectives of all three CAKN parks (U. S. Congress 1980). Wolves are important to park visitors because of the unique opportunities to view or hear wolves in Alaskan parks. While the primary objectives of wolf monitoring will be to track the distribution and abundance of wolves, a variety of accessory data will be obtained in the monitoring process that are likely to be valuable for wildlife management and research. The body of data on wolf populations in Alaska parks is of great value in developing scientific models of predator/prey systems. In heavily visited portions of the parks, managers may want to know the locations of active wolf dens and rendezvous sites so that they can be protected from disturbance. When intensive wolf harvest or wolf control take place near parks, it is important to know home range boundaries and travel patterns of wolf packs utilizing park lands. These data are used to determine and possibly mitigate impacts of wolf control activities outside the parks. Data on the genetic and morphological characteristics of wolves, obtained as a sidelight to wolf capture, are important in evaluating long-term changes in wolf populations in Alaska.

Measurable Objectives

- Locate non-radiocollared wolf packs utilizing Preserve lands by snow tracking.
- Capture and radio-collar 1 -3 individuals in each wolf pack identified in the study area.
- Determine the demography (numbers, colors, age structure) of wolf packs using Preserve lands.
- Obtain morphological measurements from captured wolves.
- Obtain genotypic data (mitochondrial and microsatellite DNA) from captured wolves.
- Obtain immunological (disease exposure) data from captured wolves.
- Define home ranges of collared wolf packs via GPS collar data and aerial telemetry.
- Determine pack size for each collared pack in fall (early winter) and spring (late winter) each biological year (May 1 – April 30).
- Define the mosaic of wolf home ranges (population area) for estimating biannual wolf densities (fall and spring of each biological year).
- Count the total number of wolves in each radio-marked pack in fall (Sept- Oct) and spring (March – April) to calculate the percentage of the annual drop in mean pack size over winter.
- Perform annual capture efforts to maintain coverage of radio collars in the population.
- Detect pack extinction and pack formation events in the population.
- Detect changes in wolf density over time
- Detect changes in wolf pack size over time
- Detect changes in wolf home range size over time.
- Detect changes in the morphological, immunological, and genetic makeup of the wolf population over time.

Methods and Materials

Methods followed the wolf monitoring protocol (Meier and Burch 2004) and include aerial radio telemetry, the use of GPS collars, and direct observation as primary techniques. Radiotelemetry and GPS provide the most effective way to identify and monitor individual packs and populations of wolves as well as to monitor natality, recruitment, causes and rates of mortality and dispersal, and predator – prey relationships (Mech et. al. 1998, Mech and Barber 2002).

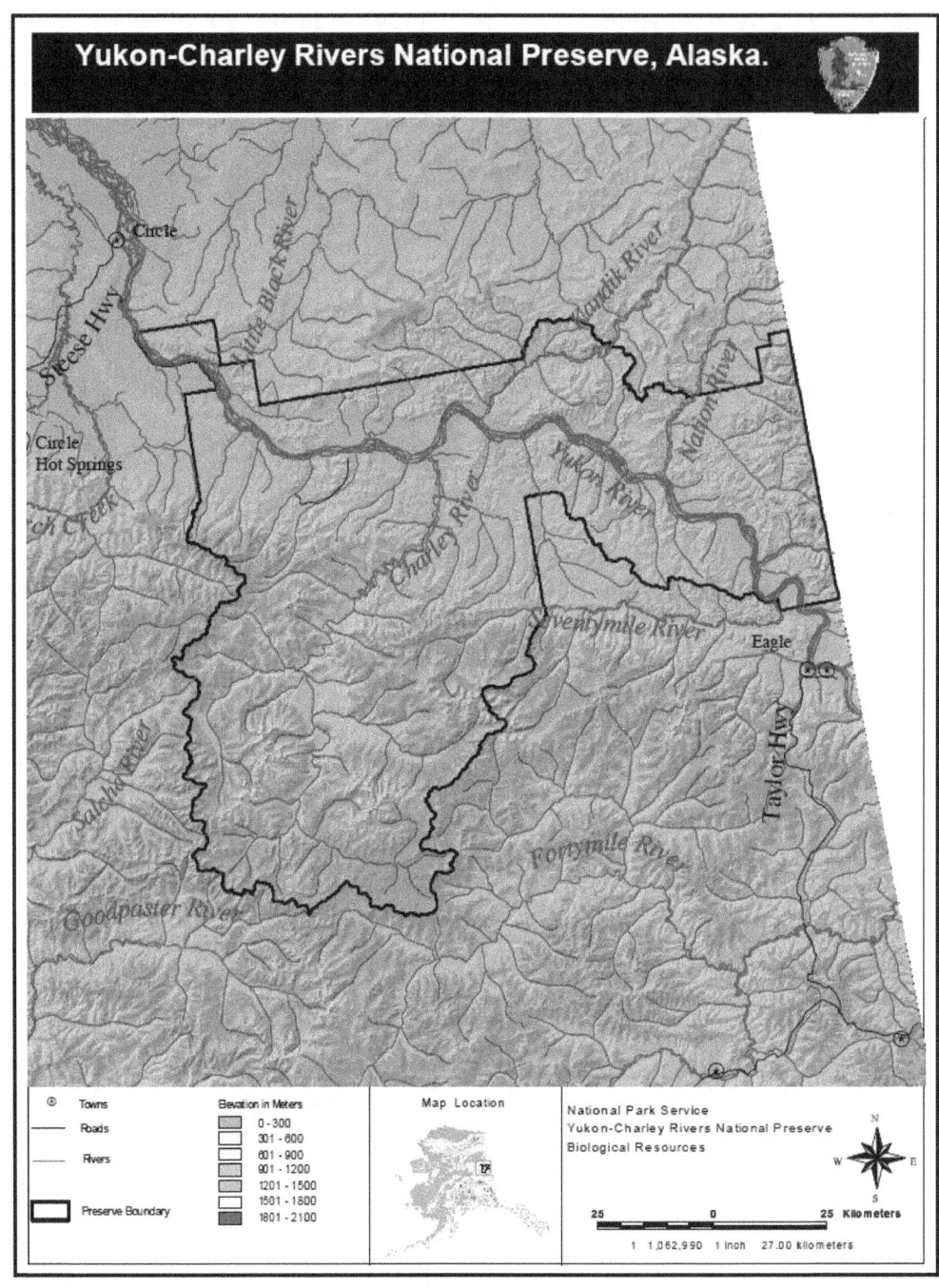

Figure 1. Wolf monitoring study area, Yukon-Charley Rivers National Preserve.

Results and Discussion

Captures and Radio Telemetry

During November 2009 and February 2010, 9 wolves were captured and radio-collared in or near YUCH, 2 of which were recaptures. Sex and age composition of captured wolves included 4 adult males, 1 male pup, 3 adult females, and 1 female pup. The capture sample is biased toward adult wolves as breeding adult wolves are specifically targeted because they are less likely to disperse. Colors of captured wolves varied widely from black to 'blue' (silver gray) to various shades of gray to white. Over the history of the project weights of captured males ranged from 70-148 lbs., (32-67 kg) averaging 108 lbs (49 kg), captured females ranged from 57-130 lbs. (26–59 kg) and averaged 90 lbs (41 kg).

We had fair snow conditions for searching for uncollared packs in 4 areas in February 2010, the Webber Creek and Nation packs were found and collared. The Webber Creek pack was killed in the ADF&G wolf control just a month after they were found and collared. In the remaining 2 areas no old tracks were seen indicating that wolf packs may not exist in areas where they once did. Local reports of few or no wolves on the Lower Kandik River from Mark Richards and Don Woodruff help confirm some of our findings.

Home range Sizes and Movements

Previous home range sizes for individual Preserve packs varied from 268 – 7067 km^2. Annual means ranged from 1639 to 3253 km^2 with a grand mean of 2295 km^2, which is larger than found in most other wolf studies (Figures 2-5) (Burch 2002). With the advent of GPS collars, the annual number of locations per pack has increased nearly 10 fold and with it an increase in individual home range size (Burch et al. 2005). Home range of packs containing one GPS collar were more than 35% larger than those found using conventional aerial telemetry (Figure 7).

In years prior to the common use of GPS collars, home range size was measured for each radiomarked pack where more than 20 locations were available in a 2 year time block. This was an attempt to overcome the problem of home range size being dependent on the sample size of locations (when calculated using Minimum Convex Polygons (MCP)). Even with this doubling of sample size the relationship still holds ($r^2 = 19.4$, $P = 0.00017$, n = 67) (Figure 8) and MPC home range size was still dependent on the number of locations (White and Garrott 1990). With the advent of GPS collars, 1 biological year of locations is used, but the problem of home range size being dependent on sample size looks like it may still exist even with 300 locations per year, although the effect is much smaller. Starting this year we are looking into kernel estimates as a possible solution to this problem (Worton 1989).

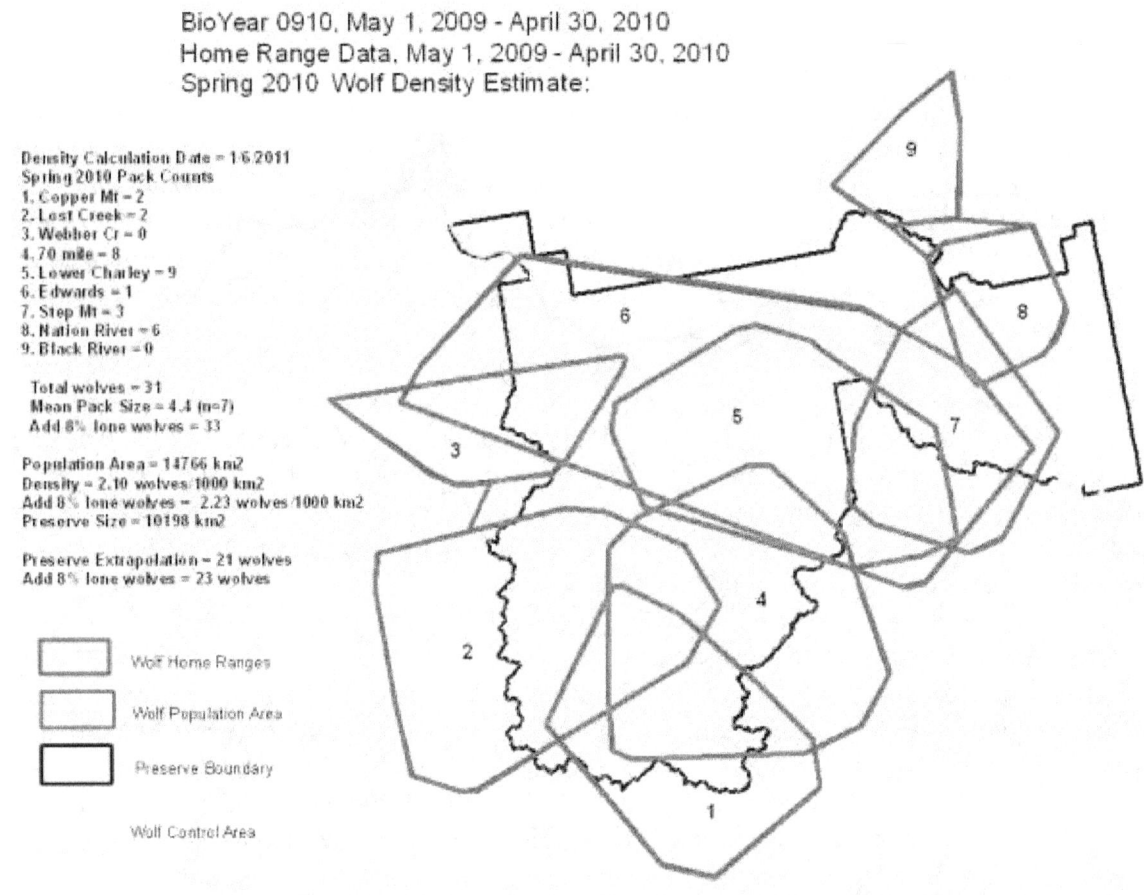

BioYear 0910, May 1, 2009 - April 30, 2010
Home Range Data, May 1, 2009 - April 30, 2010
Spring 2010 Wolf Density Estimate:

Density Calculation Date = 1/6/2011
Spring 2010 Pack Counts
1. Copper Mt = 2
2. Lost Creek = 2
3. Webber Cr = 0
4. 70 mile = 8
5. Lower Charley = 9
6. Edwards = 1
7. Step Mt = 3
8. Nation River = 6
9. Black River = 0

Total wolves = 31
Mean Pack Size = 4.4 (n=7)
Add 8% lone wolves = 33

Population Area = 14766 km2
Density = 2.10 wolves/1000 km2
Add 8% lone wolves = 2.23 wolves/1000 km2
Preserve Size = 10198 km2

Preserve Extrapolation = 21 wolves
Add 8% lone wolves = 23 wolves

Wolf Home Ranges

Wolf Population Area

Preserve Boundary

Wolf Control Area

Figure 2. Spring 2010 map of individual pack home ranges, pack counts, and density calculation. Minimum convex polygons are used to delineate pack home ranges.

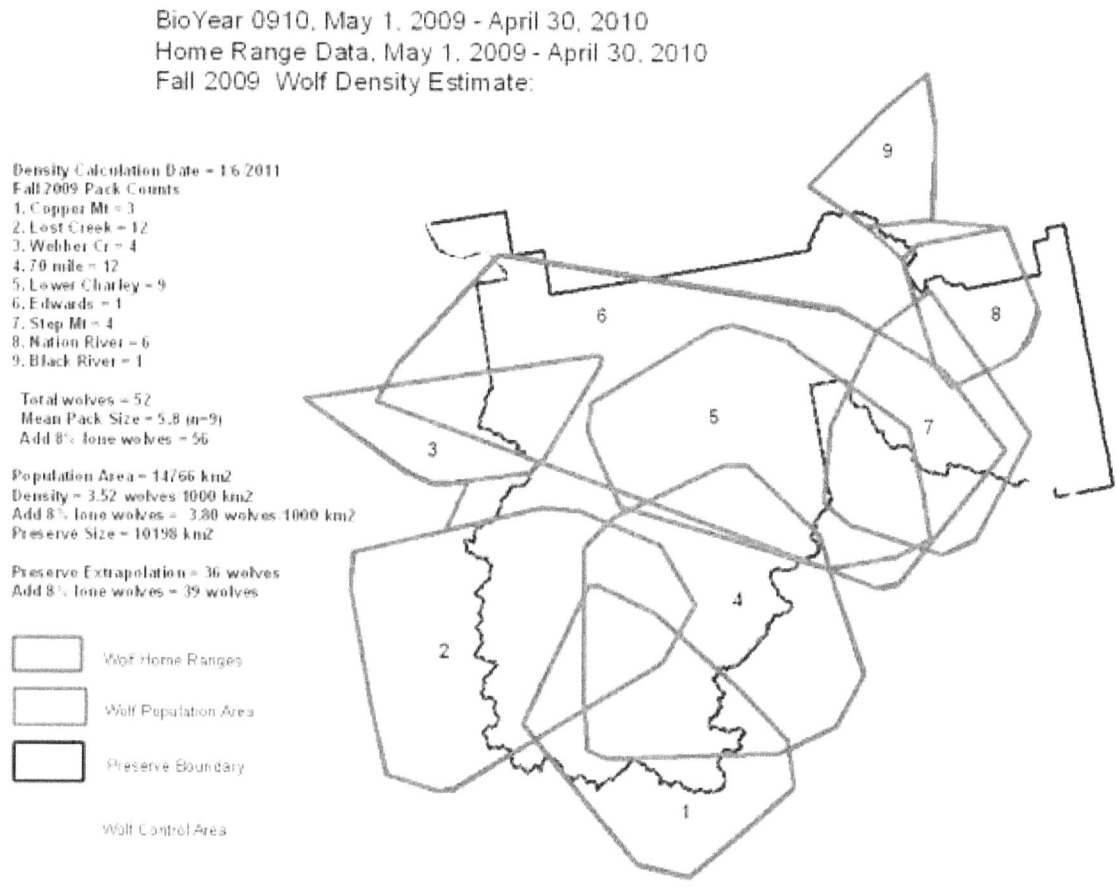

BioYear 0910, May 1, 2009 - April 30, 2010
Home Range Data, May 1, 2009 - April 30, 2010
Fall 2009 Wolf Density Estimate:

Density Calculation Date = 1.6.2011
Fall 2009 Pack Counts
1. Copper Mt = 3
2. Lost Creek = 12
3. Webber Cr = 4
4. 70 mile = 12
5. Lower Charley = 9
6. Edwards = 1
7. Step Mt = 4
8. Nation River = 6
9. Black River = 1

Total wolves = 52
Mean Pack Size = 5.8 (n=9)
Add 8% lone wolves = 56

Population Area = 14766 km2
Density = 3.52 wolves 1000 km2
Add 8% lone wolves = 3.80 wolves 1000 km2
Preserve Size = 10198 km2

Preserve Extrapolation = 36 wolves
Add 8% lone wolves = 39 wolves

Wolf Home Ranges

Wolf Population Area

Preserve Boundary

Wolf Control Area

Figure 3. Fall 2009 map of individual pack home ranges, pack counts, and density calculation. Minimum convex polygons are used to delineate pack home ranges.

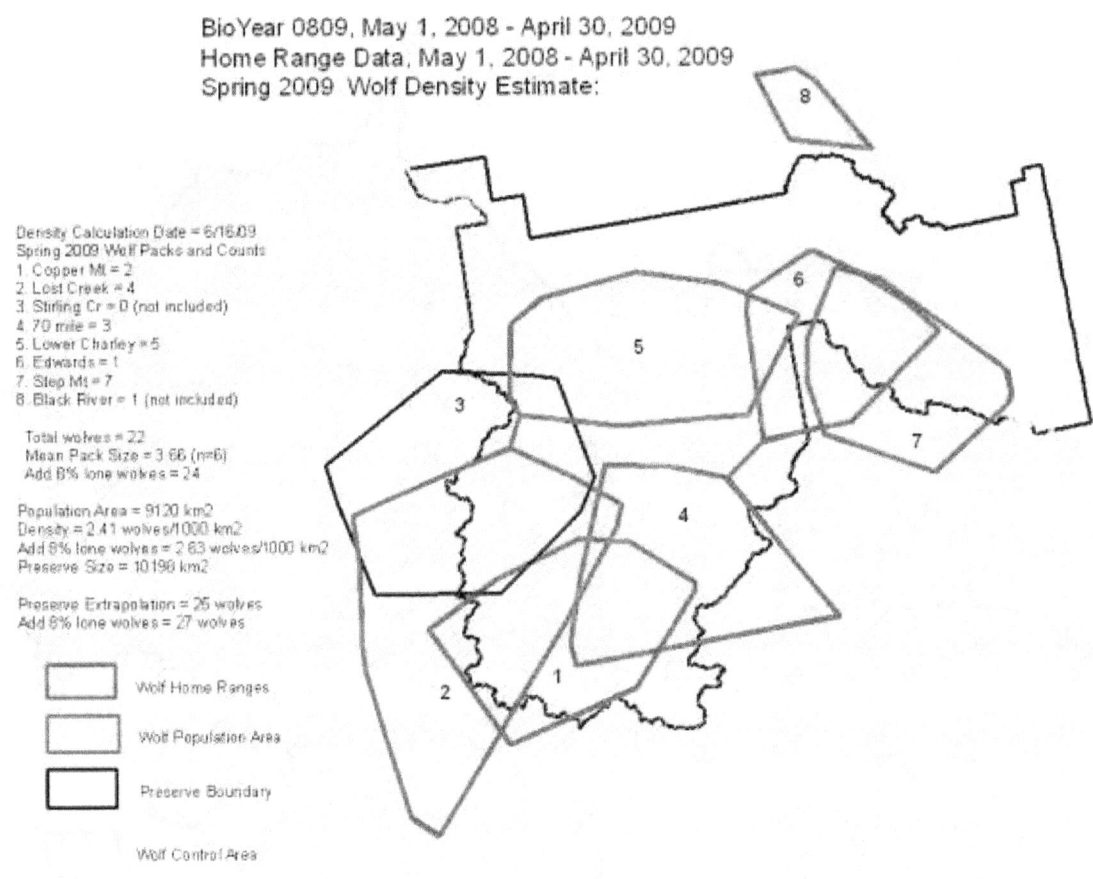

BioYear 0809, May 1, 2008 - April 30, 2009
Home Range Data, May 1, 2008 - April 30, 2009
Spring 2009 Wolf Density Estimate:

Density Calculation Date = 6/16/09
Spring 2009 Wolf Packs and Counts
1. Copper Mt = 2
2. Lost Creek = 4
3. Stirling Cr = 0 (not included)
4. 70 mile = 3
5. Lower Charley = 5
6. Edwards = 1
7. Step Mt = 7
8. Black River = 1 (not included)

Total wolves = 22
Mean Pack Size = 3.66 (n=6)
Add 8% lone wolves = 24

Population Area = 9120 km2
Density = 2.41 wolves/1000 km2
Add 8% lone wolves = 2.63 wolves/1000 km2
Preserve Size = 10190 km2

Preserve Extrapolation = 25 wolves
Add 8% lone wolves = 27 wolves

Wolf Home Ranges

Wolf Population Area

Preserve Boundary

Wolf Control Area

Figure 4. Spring 2009 map of individual pack home ranges, pack counts, and density calculation. Minimum convex polygons are used to delineate pack home ranges.

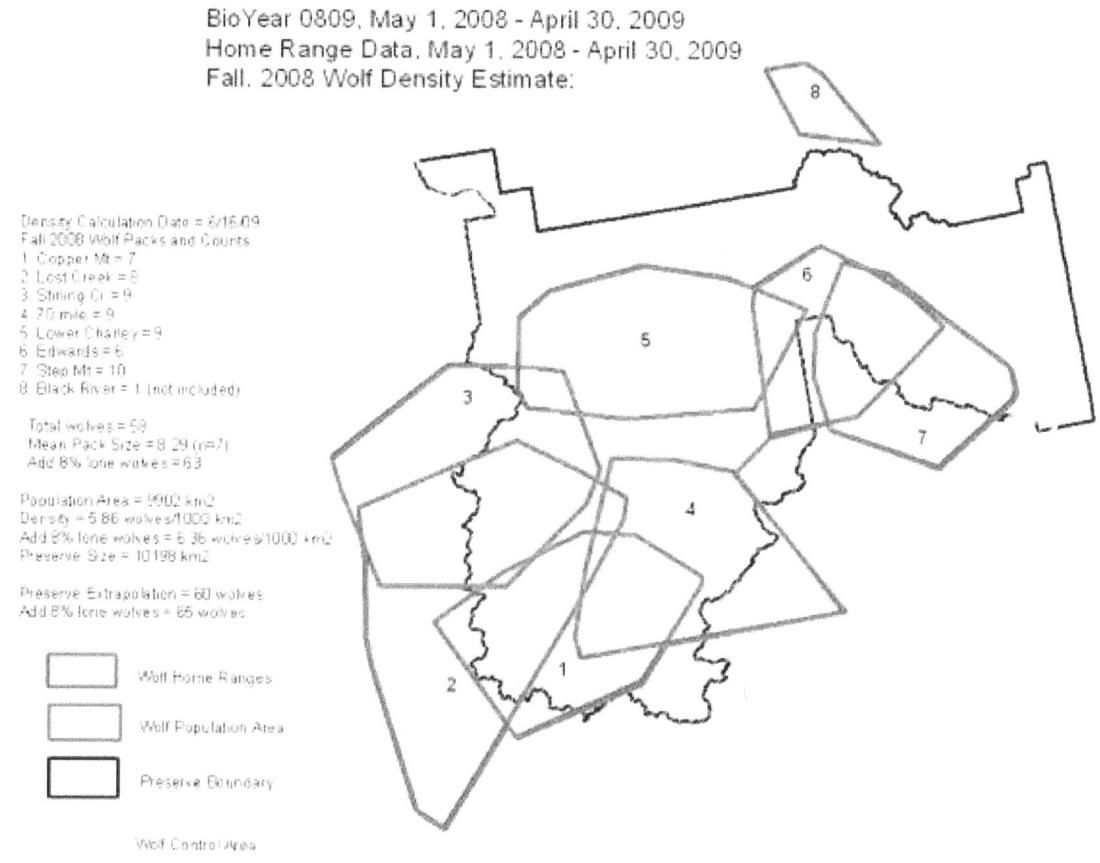

BioYear 0809, May 1, 2008 - April 30, 2009
Home Range Data, May 1, 2008 - April 30, 2009
Fall, 2008 Wolf Density Estimate:

Density Calculation Date = 6/16/09
Fall 2008 Wolf Packs and Counts
1. Copper Mt = 7
2. Lost Creek = 8
3. Stirling Cr = 9
4. 70 mile = 9
5. Lower Charley = 9
6. Edwards = 6
7. Step Mt = 10
8. Black River = 1 (not included)

Total wolves = 59
Mean Pack Size = 8.29 (n=7)
Add 8% lone wolves = 63

Population Area = 9902 km2
Density = 5.88 wolves/1000 km2
Add 8% lone wolves = 6.36 wolves/1000 km2
Preserve Size = 10198 km2

Preserve Extrapolation = 60 wolves
Add 8% lone wolves = 65 wolves

Wolf Home Ranges

Wolf Population Area

Preserve Boundary

Wolf Control Area

Figure 5. Fall 2008 map of individual pack home ranges, pack counts, and density calculation. Minimum convex polygons are used to delineate pack home ranges.

Pack Sizes, Density and Population Estimate

A new measure of wolf population change was developed this year to help make management decisions quickly at any time through the year. Accurate density estimates require a full biological year (May 1 – April 30) of location/home range data to calculate density estimates consistently from one year to the next. As a result density estimates calculated earlier in the year must be based on the previous year's location data and what location data is available so far from the current year. This can result in erroneous or inaccurate density estimates. The new measure in wolf population change utilizes the drop in counts of wolves of radio-marked packs from fall (September/October) to Spring (March and April) or at any time in between. During biological year 09-10 the counts dropped from 52 to 31 wolves, a decline of 40% (or 41% by averages) which is outside the range of 14 previous years of data (Tables 1 and 2).

These data were some of the inputs in a Structured Decision-Making (SDM) model (SDM fact sheet, U.S. Fish & Wildlife Service, October 2008) used by Superintendent Greg Dudgeon to decide to temporarily close the sport hunting and trapping seasons in Yukon-Charley in spring 2010, while keeping the subsistence harvest of wolves open. The decision was based on the fact that, although the spring 2010 wolf density looked as though it was going to be close to past spring densities (Figure 12), the actual count of total number of wolves in collared packs dropped 40% (41% by averages), from 52 wolves in the fall to 31 wolves by February, plus the added threat of more wolves with home ranges in the Preserve being killed in the State's wolf control program outside the Yukon-Charley boundary.

Table 1. History of changes in average pack size for collared packs between fall and spring. This only includes packs where data are available for both seasons. The two years highlighted in red indicate years where predator control activities may have affected population changes and are not included the 'normal' range (green).

Winter	Fall	Spring	Percent Drop
1993 - 1994	4.5	4.0	0.11
1994 - 1995	7.0	5.0	0.29
1995 - 1996	7.3	6.0	0.18
1996 - 1997	10.3	7.7	0.25
1997 - 1998	8.0	5.6	0.30
1998 - 1999	6.7	5.7	0.15
1999 - 2000	8.2	5.5	0.33
2000 - 2001	7.9	5.3	0.33
2001 - 2002	8.8	6.5	0.26
2002 - 2003	8.6	7.1	0.17
2003 - 2004	9.2	6.7	0.27
2004 - 2005	8.7	5.5	0.37
2005 - 2006	7.4	5.2	0.30
2006 - 2007	4.9	2.4	0.51
2007 - 2008	5.8	4.0	0.31
2008 - 2009	7.1	2.9	0.59
Range (Normal)	4.5 - 10.3	3.7 - 7.7	**0.11 - 0.37**

Table 2. Change in pack counts and the percent drop in size of radio collared wolf packs in Yukon-Charley Rivers National Preserve from Fall 2009 to Spring 2010. The 41% is the average of the percent drops in the 9 packs, a little higher than the percent drop of the average (38%) because it weights the smaller packs more.

| | | Pack | Counts | |
| | | 2009 | 2010 | |
	Pack	Fall	Spring	Percent Drop
1	Edwards Cr	1	1	0%
2	Lower Charley	9	9	0%
3	Step Mt	4	3	25%
4	70mile	12	8	33%
5	Copper Mt	3	2	33%
6	Black River	1	0	100%
7	Lost Creek	12	2	83%
8	Webber Cr[1]	4+	0	100%
9	Nation[1]	6+	6	0%
	Total wolves	52	31	40%
	Average	5.8	3.4	41%[2]

[1] The Webber Creek and Nation packs were not collared in Fall 2009, so the fall pack sizes shown are numbers seen later in the winter, and the percent drop in numbers in those packs could have been larger than shown. [2] The 41% is the average of the percent drops in the 9 packs, a little higher than the percent drop of the average (38%) because it weights the smaller packs more.

Fall mean pack sizes have ranged from 4.3 to 9.1, with a 17 year average (1993 – 2009) of 7.1 (Figure 10). The wolf population in the area continues to fluctuate and is likely responding to changes in the accessibility and vulnerability to predation of Fortymile Caribou. From 1993 – 2001 the increasing trend in mean pack size was significant (r^2=0.59, P=0.015), however from 2002 on it levels out and then drops in 2005 (Figure 10). Wolf densities follow the same trends as mean pack sizes (Figures 13 & 14). Most recently, the population hit an all-time low density of 1.6 wolves/1000 km^2 in spring 2007, then rebounded to almost 2.5 in spring 2008. The fall 2008 wolf density estimate was the highest calculated since the study began in 1993 at 5.86 wolves/1000 km^2. This was followed by the largest drop in population size to a spring 2009 density of 2.41 wolves/1000 km^2. This dramatic drop (59% when measured by mean pack size, Table 1) seems as though it must be related to the States wolf control efforts, however this is not reflected in the fates of the sample of radio collared wolves, or by what could be learned from word of mouth. The Fall 2009 density of 3.52 was below the overall average of 4.18, and the Spring 2010 density of 2.10 was also below the long term average of 2.75. Fall densities are measured when pack size is at its highest and densities are at the greatest for the biological year and follow the same overall trend pattern as Mean pack size (Figure 10). Pack sizes are actually greater right after pups are born in May. However, we cannot reliably count all the pups from airplanes in all the packs until September or October when the pups are traveling consistently with the rest of the pack and there might be some snow on the ground to increase sightability.

Kernel Home Range Analysis

This year a first try was made to use Kernel Analysis (Worton, 1989) to measure the population area as opposed to Minimum Convex Polygons (MCPs) (Figure 6). The hope is in developing a more objective and consistent method for measuring annual home ranges and population area to be used in calculating wolf density estimates. One problem with MCPs is their dependence on sample size of locations, a second problem is the subjective decisions needed to remove outliers where wolves disperse or temporarily leave their homerange on forays. A more in depth discussion of the problems of calculating wolf density estimates from radio telemetry data can be found in Burch et. al. (1995). Using the 75% Kernel for Spring 2010 produces a population area of 13909 km^2 and a density of 2.23 wolves/1000km^2 which is slightly higher than the standard minimum convex polygon (MCP) method (Figure 6 vs. Figure 2).

Kernel BioYear 0910, May 1, 2009 - April 30, 2010
Home Range Data, May 1, 2009 - April 30, 2010
Spring 2010 Wolf Density Estimate:

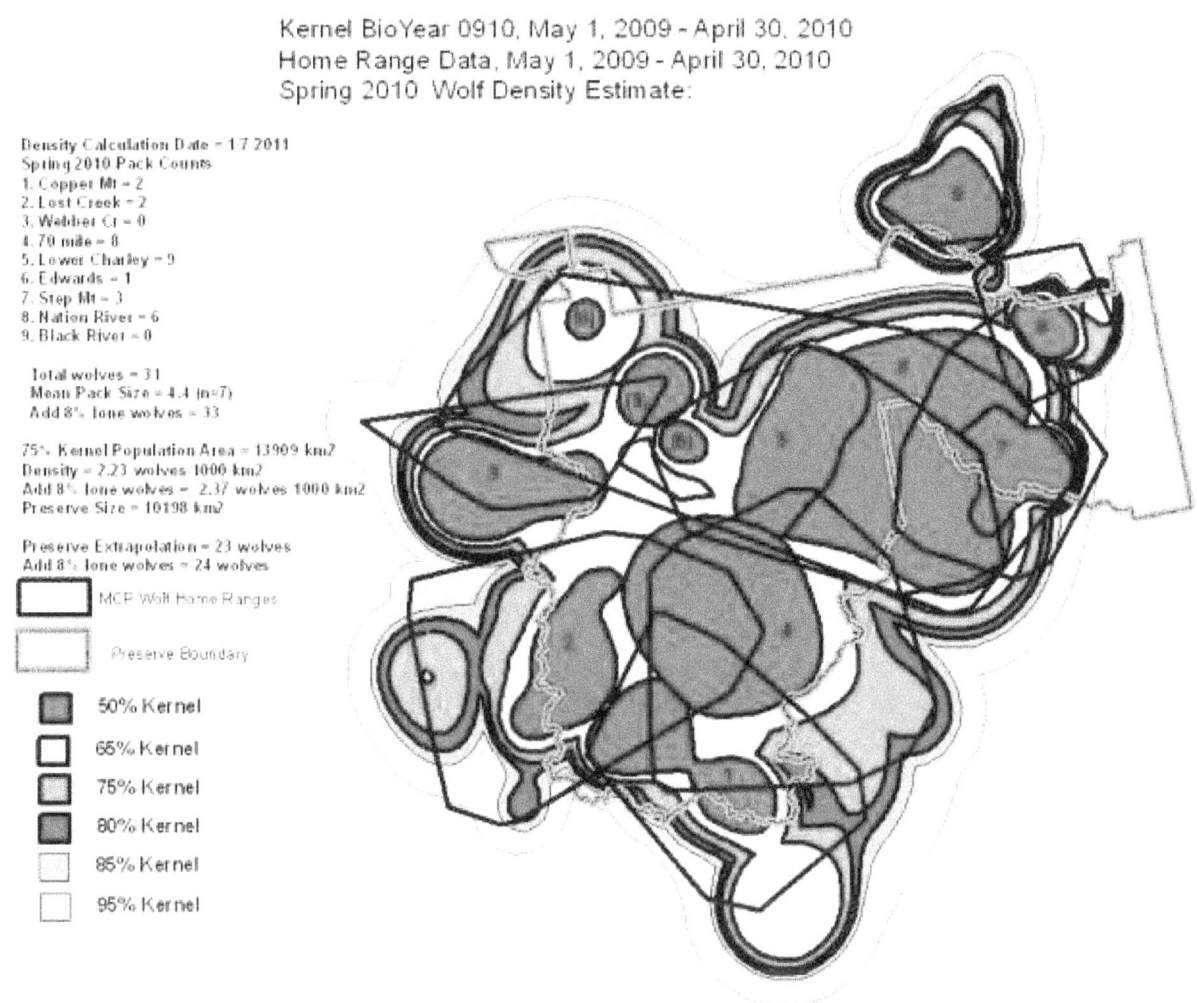

Density Calculation Date = 1 7 2011
Spring 2010 Pack Counts
1. Copper Mt = 2
2. Lost Creek = 2
3. Webber Cr = 0
4. 70 mile = 8
5. Lower Charley = 9
6. Edwards = 1
7. Step Mt = 3
8. Nation River = 6
9. Black River = 0

 Total wolves = 31
 Mean Pack Size = 4.4 (n=7)
 Add 8% lone wolves = 33

75% Kernel Population Area = 13909 km2
Density = 2.23 wolves 1000 km2
Add 8% lone wolves = 2.37 wolves 1000 km2
Preserve Size = 10198 km2

Preserve Extrapolation = 23 wolves
Add 8% lone wolves = 24 wolves

MCP Wolf Home Ranges

Preserve Boundary

50% Kernel

65% Kernel

75% Kernel

80% Kernel

85% Kernel

95% Kernel

Figure 6. 50% - 95% Kernel home ranges of the Spring 2010 population area superimposed with the minimum convex polygons (MCP) of each pack. The Density calculation is made from the 75% Kernel.

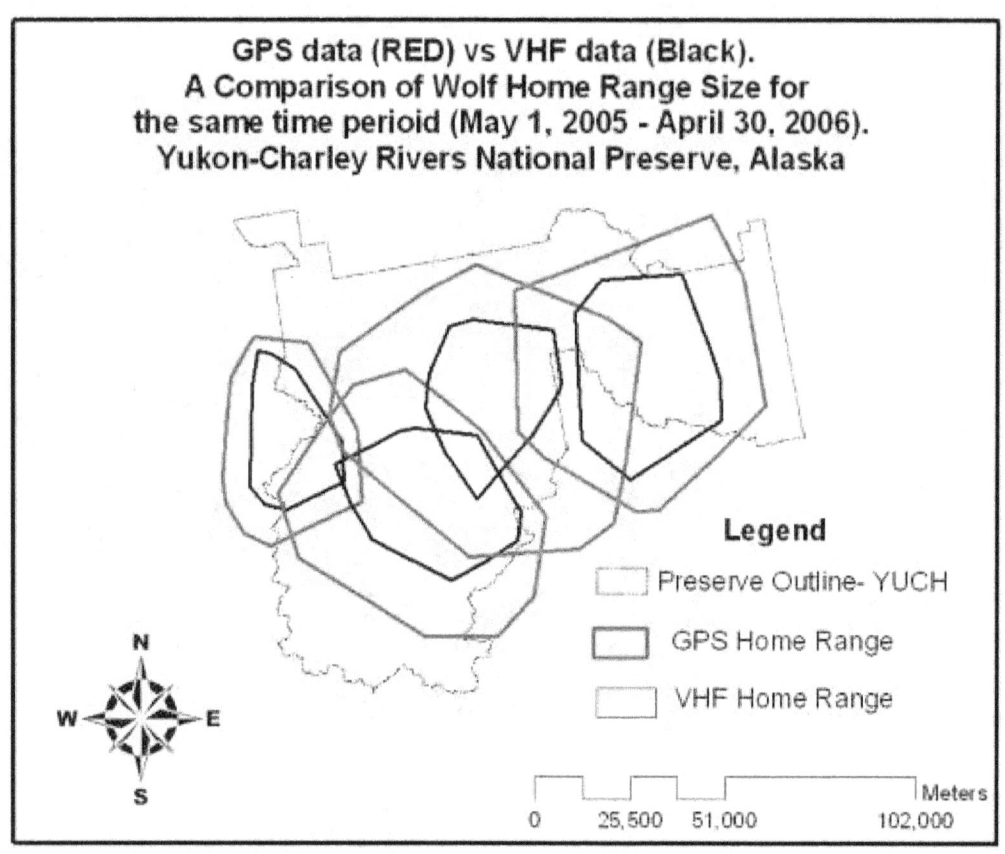

Figure 7. Wolf home ranges measured with GPS collars are over 35% larger on average than those from conventional aerial radiotelemetry (VHF) when measured over the same time period. Average GPS home range = 3322 km^2. Average VHF home Range = 1211 km^2. Not all home ranges depicted for clarity.

Home Range Size vs Number of Locations

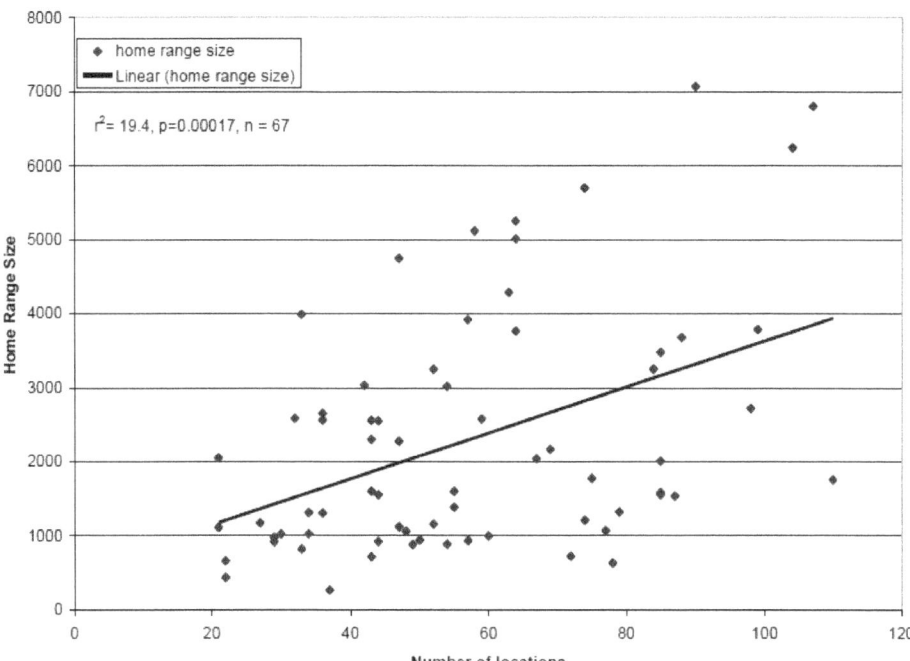

Figure 8. Wolf home range size vs. number of locations showing that home ranges calculated using minimum convex polygons are dependent on sample size of locations. Yukon-Charley Rivers National Preserve, Alaska, 1993 – 2005.

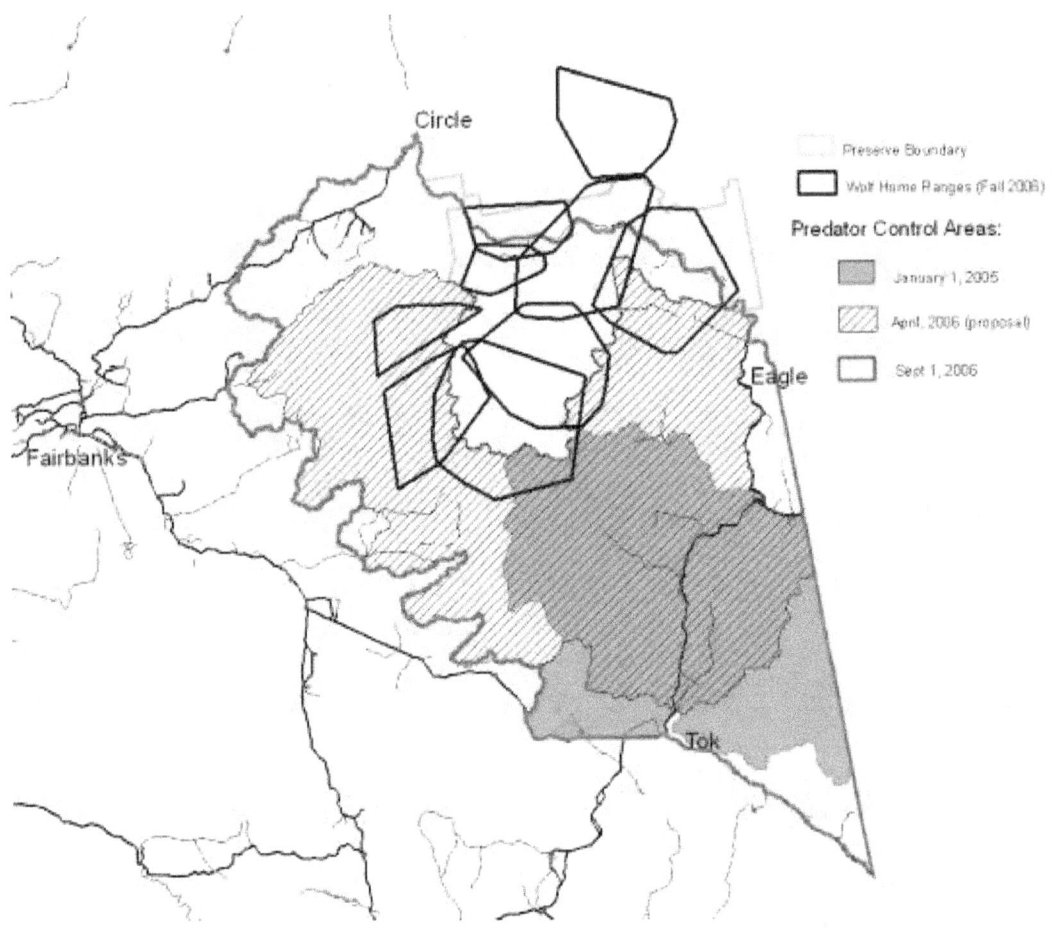

Figure 9. Map depicting the recent history and progression of wolf control boundaries relative to YUCH. UYTPCA (Upper Yukon Tanana Predator Control Area) = 48,550 km^2 (red line) has been in effect since Sept 2006.

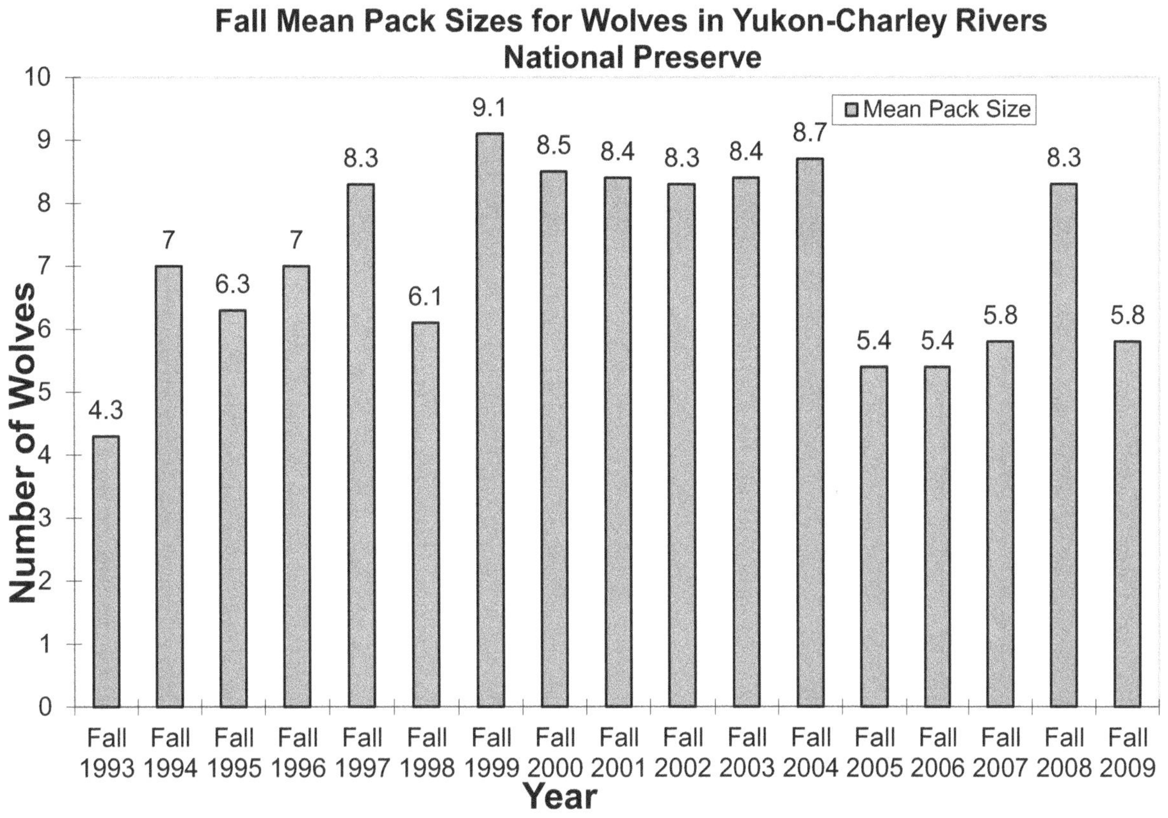

Fall Mean Pack Sizes for Wolves in Yukon-Charley Rivers National Preserve

Figure 10. Trend in wolf population using Fall mean pack size, Average = 7.1. Yukon-Charley Rivers National Preserve 1993 – 2009.

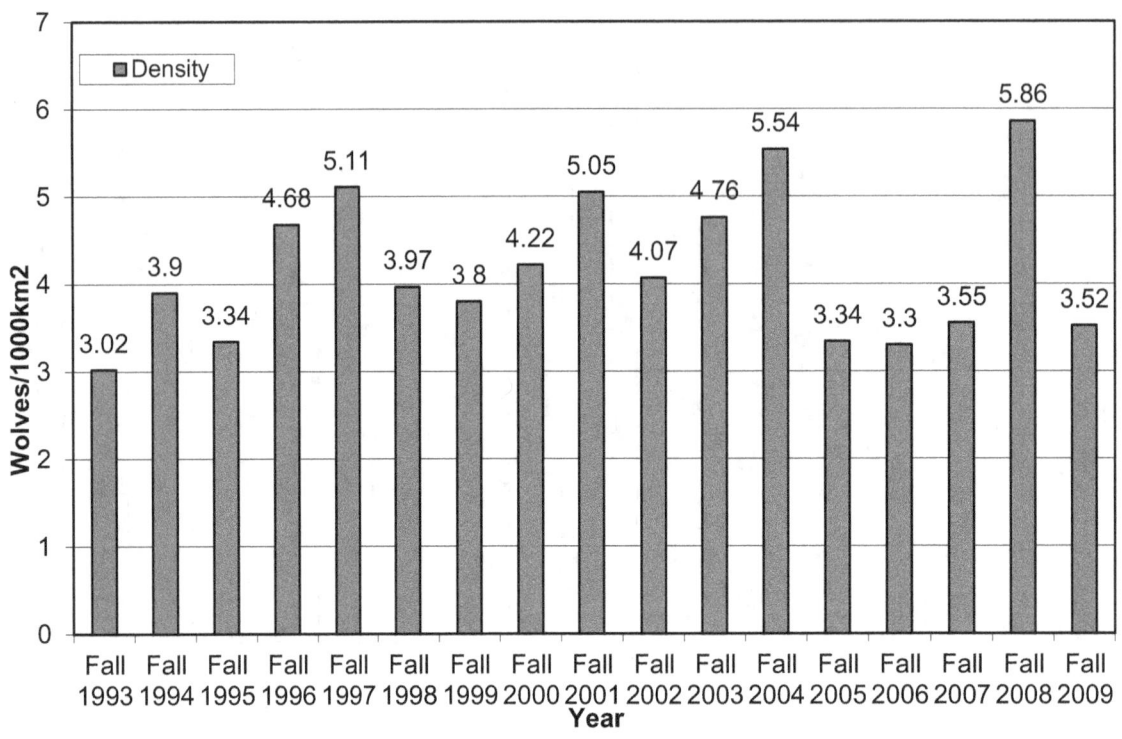

Figure 11. Fall wolf densities (wolves/1000 km^2) in YUCH 1993 – 2009. (Average=4.18)

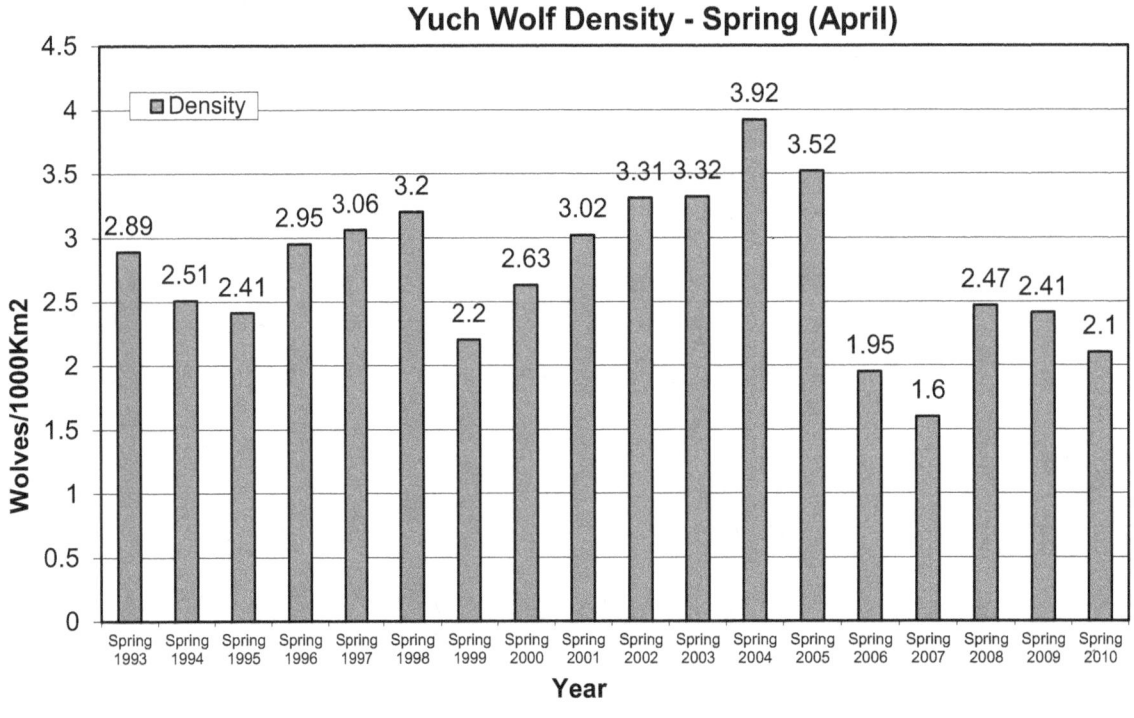

Figure 12. Spring wolf densities (wolves/1000km^2) in YUCH, 1993 – 2010 (Average= 2.75).

Wolf Population Estimate vs Number of Locations

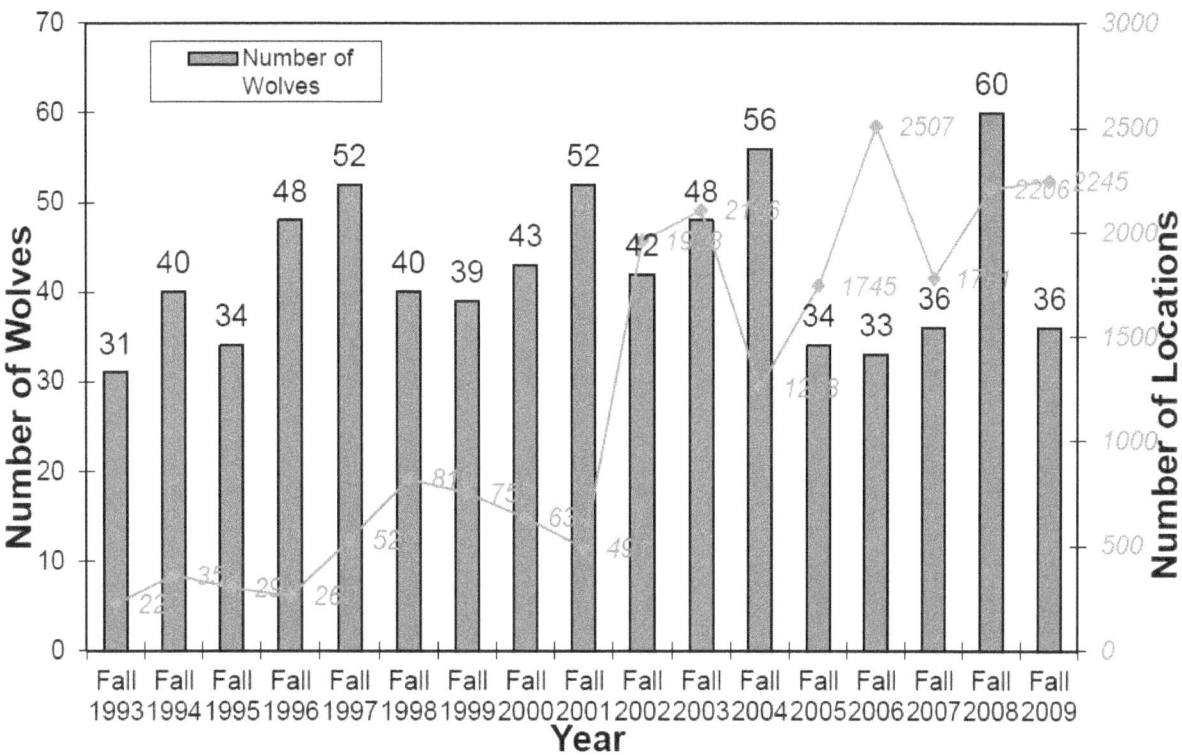

Figure 13. Comparing fall wolf population (extrapolating fall densities to the YUCH Preserve boundary to estimate the number of wolves in the Preserve at any given time) with location counts.

Fortymile Caribou

In 1920 biologist Olaus Murie estimated the Forty Mile Caribou Herd (FCH) to number 568,000 caribou, and the herd ranged from Whitehorse, Yukon to the White Mountains north of Fairbanks (Murie 1935). It is difficult to know how accurate Murie's estimate was as he estimated how many caribou crossed a 1 mile stretch of the Steese Highway in one day and then multiplies that number for a forty mile stretch for 20 days, which is what was reported by others to be the place and time that the herd crossed the road (Murie 1935). In the 1930s the herd population dropped to an estimated 10,000 to 20,000 caribou. The cause of this dramatic decline is unknown but suspicions include overharvest, and food limitations due to range depletion and fires, or other wide spread phenomena. Predation was not considered a causal factor (Valkenburg et al 1994).

During the 1940s and 1950s the herd increased again to perhaps as many as 50,000. From an estimated 50,000 animals in 1963 the herd size dropped dramatically again to 6000 animals in 1973 and Fortymile caribou stopped crossing the Steese Highway. The cause of this decline was attributed to a combination of overharvest, deep snow conditions, and predation by wolves and bears. Starting in 1976, the herd began to increase slowly to over 22,000 by 1990 and was roughly stable at 22000 – 23000 through 1995 (Valkenburg et al 1994, Boertje and Gardner 1996). In 1994 the Fortymile Planning Team was formed and plans for wolf reductions and reduced human harvest on caribou were made. From 1995 through 2002, the herd grew to nearly 45,000 animals (Boertje and Gardner 1996, Jeff Gross, Tok area biologist, Pers. Comm.) where it remained roughly stable through 2006. The most recent photo census of June 2007 produced a population estimate of 38,364 (Jeff Gross, Tok area biologist, Pers. Comm.) (Figure 14). No photo census occurred in 2008 due to cool/rainy weather resulting in the caribou not grouping up enough to conduct the census.

The drop in wolf numbers in 2005 – 2007 does not correlate well with the roughly stable caribou population during the same time (Figure 14). Low snowfall winters at this time may have allowed the caribou (and moose) to be less vulnerable to wolf predation, thereby causing an increase in wolf dispersal and natural mortality and a decrease in pup production and survival (Figure 15), culminating in a drop in the wolf population. Human Harvest levels at this time were lower than the 23 year annual average of about 7 wolves harvested within the Preserve (Figures 16 &17) and likely played no role in the drop in wolf numbers.

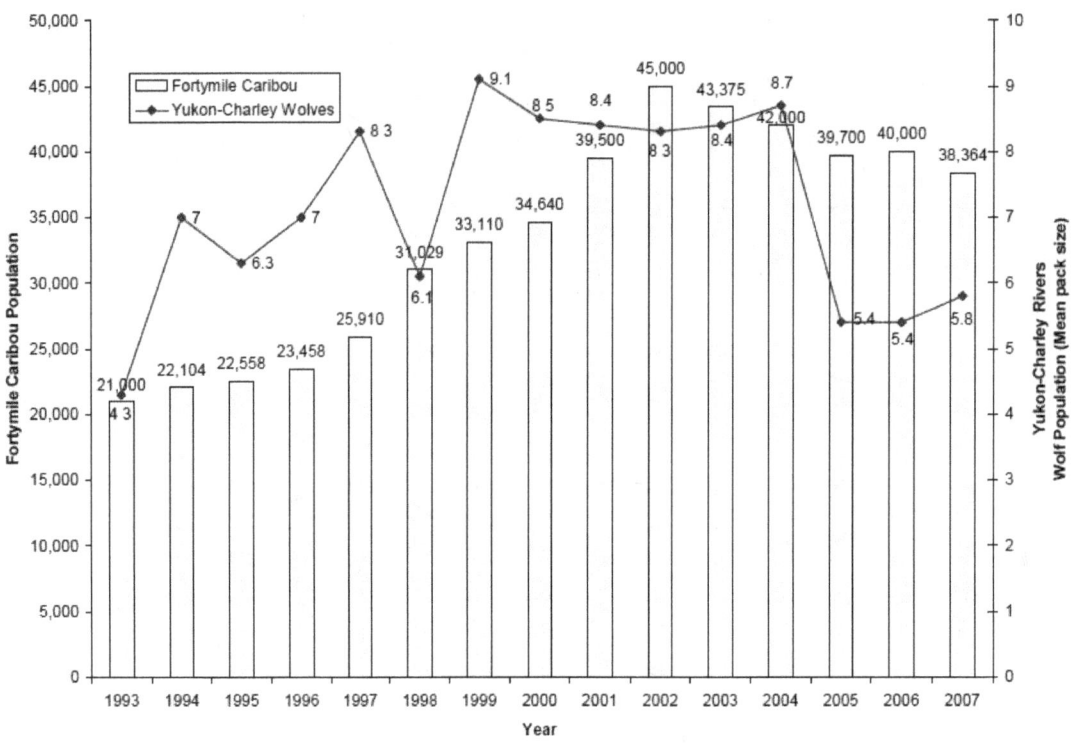

Figure 14. Trend in population change for the Fortymile Caribou Herd (trend in photo census counts) and wolves (in mean pack size) in Yukon-Charley Rivers National Preserve, Alaska, 1993 – 2007.

Natality

Pup production and survival to fall is illustrated in Figure 15. The counts of pups are from September - November of each year when the pups are still small enough to distinguish from adults from an airplane. Likely there are more pups born in May and some pup mortality occurs between May and September, so these are minimum counts. The cause of the drop in pup production and/or survival in 2004 and 2005 is unknown but correlates well with the overall drop in population size from 2004 to 2006 (Figures 11, 12, 13 & 14).

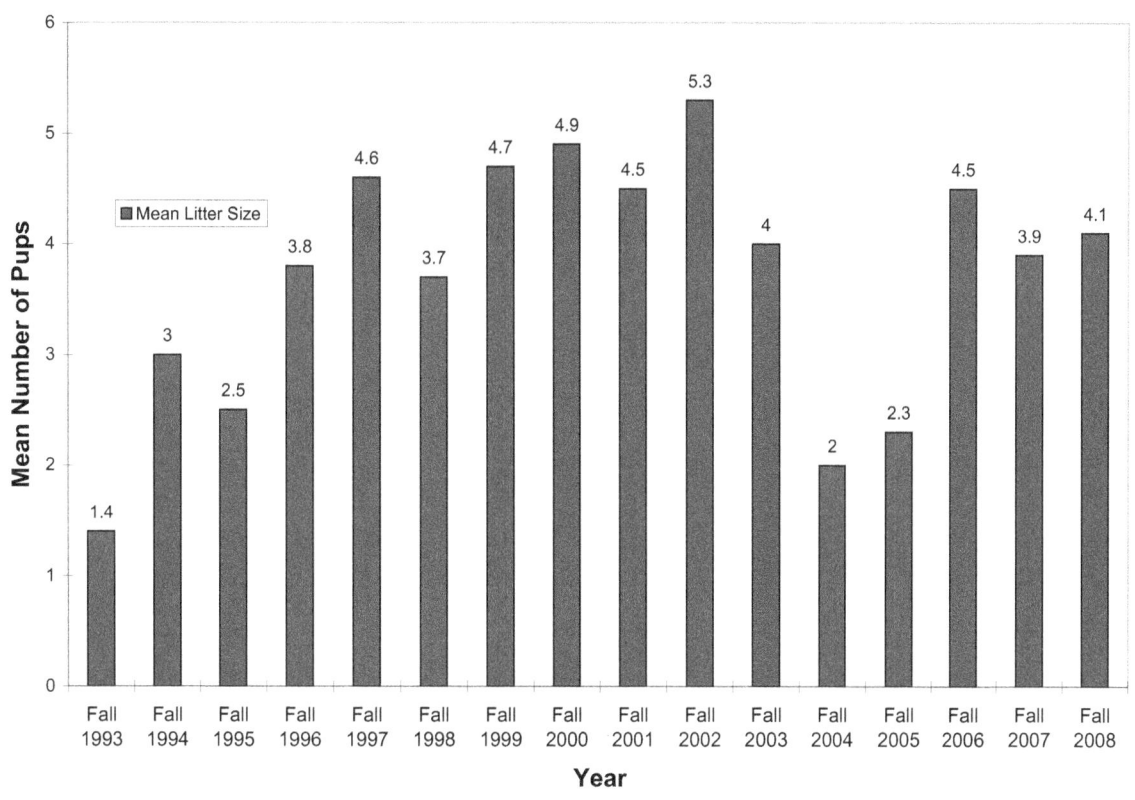

Figure 15. Trend in Pup production and survival to fall (September/October mean litter sizes).

Mortality

All preserve packs travel outside the boundaries of YUCH, many extensively (Figure 2 - 6). As a result, regulations regarding wolf management outside YUCH's boundary affect the entire wolf population utilizing Preserve lands. This idea is well illustrated by The Alaska Board of Game's series of decisions to conduct wolf control up against most of YUCH's boundary south of the Yukon River (Figure 2 – 6, 9). However, winters 2006-07 and 2007-08 had poor conditions for snow tracking wolves, resulting in very few wolves being killed in the Fortymile Control efforts (58 in 2005-06, 13 in 2006–07, and 27 in 2007-08) far below the goal of reducing the entire population to somewhere between 88 - 103 wolves.

The situation changed some last winter (2008-09) where good snow tracking conditions existed for much of the area resulting in 49 wolves being shot from permitted fixed-wing airplanes. Furthermore, ADF&G decided to shoot wolves from helicopters March 14 – 19, 2009 throughout the Upper Yukon Tanana Predator Control Area (UYTPC), excluding YUCH. 84 wolves were shot from a helicopter in this portion of the control effort, however none of the killed wolves were from radiocollared packs that utilize YUCH lands (Figure 16), and 87 wolves were harvested by conventional hunting and trapping in the UYTPCA. This adds up to 220 wolves killed within UYTPCA for the 2008-09 season.

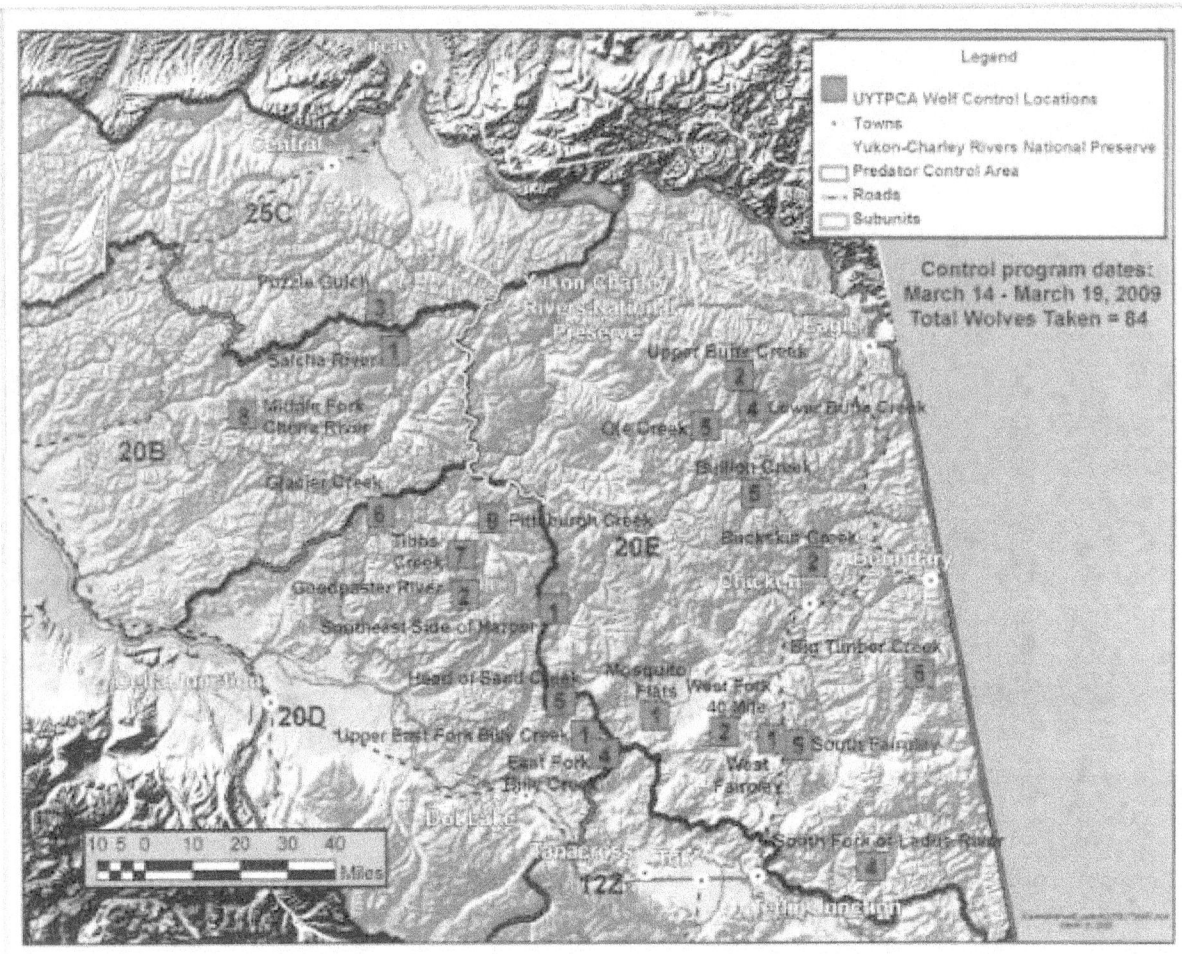

Figure 16. 2009 UYTPCA map of the location and number of wolves killed by ADF&G shooting from a helicopter. No wolves from radio collared packs utilizing YUCH lands were known to have been killed via this method. Map was created and provided to NPS courtesy of ADF&G, Fairbanks, March 25, 2009.

2010 ADF&G predator control in the UYTPCA

During this past winter (2009 – 2010) ten wolves were shot from fixed wing aircraft and 15 were shot from helicopters by ADF&G in the UYTPCA, conventional hunting and trapping usually averaged about 65, so about 90 wolves were kill in the control area last winter, considerably fewer than last years 220.

On 17 March 2010, during the helicopter control efforts by ADFG staff, all four wolves of the newly collared Webber Creek pack were shot from a helicopter. The 2 collared wolves were mistakenly shot because ADF&G staff thought the collars they saw on the wolves prior to shooting them were not working. This was incorrect. Several weeks earlier ADF&G were given the frequencies of all the Yuch wolf collars and a receiver to track them with. NPS was told ADF&G chose to transcribe those frequencies from the NPS flight sheet they were given, and inadvertently left off the frequencies of the 2 Webber Creek wolves. This resulted in the ADF&G staff in the monitoring airplane not having all the frequencies and could not hear the signals from the Webber Creek collars, thus assuming the collars seen from the helicopter were not functioning. Based on this information the helicopter crew decided to shoot the 2 collared wolves in addition to the 2 uncollared wolves in the Webber Creek Pack.

22

Fates of collared wolves

Fates of a sample of 123 radiocollared wolves (from the beginning of the project in 1993) is illustrated in Figure 17. Although the sample of collared wolves is not representative of the population, they do give a good idea of what happens to most wolves in the Yuch population. About 20% are trapped or shot within the preserve boundary (or near it). The hunting season was extended in 2008 and now runs from August 10 – May 31 with a bag limit of 5 wolves south of the Yukon, and 10 wolves north of the Yukon (no limit for trapping). Even with these liberal regulations few wolves are harvested in or near YUCH most winters. Based on ADF&G sealing records, human harvest of wolves from within the preserve (via conventional trapping and hunting methods) has averaged about 6.7 wolves per year over the past 26 years (Figure 18). This harvest is 14% of the maximum fall Yuch wolf population over an 18 year average (46.61 wolves each fall which includes an added 8% for lone wolves) and probably has had little impact on YUCH's wolf population.

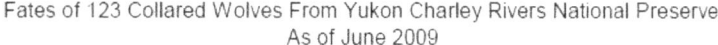

Fates of 123 Collared Wolves From Yukon Charley Rivers National Preserve
As of June 2009

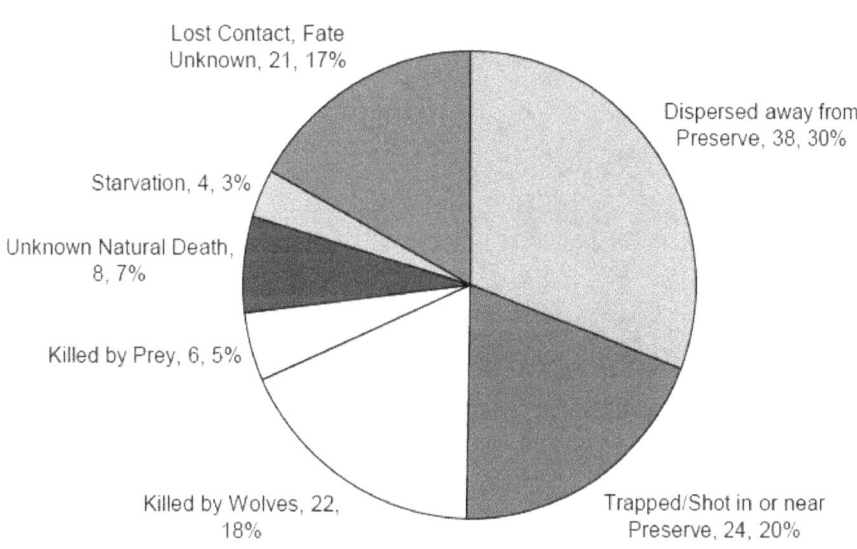

Figure 17. Fates of collared wolves in and around YUCH, 1993 – 2009.

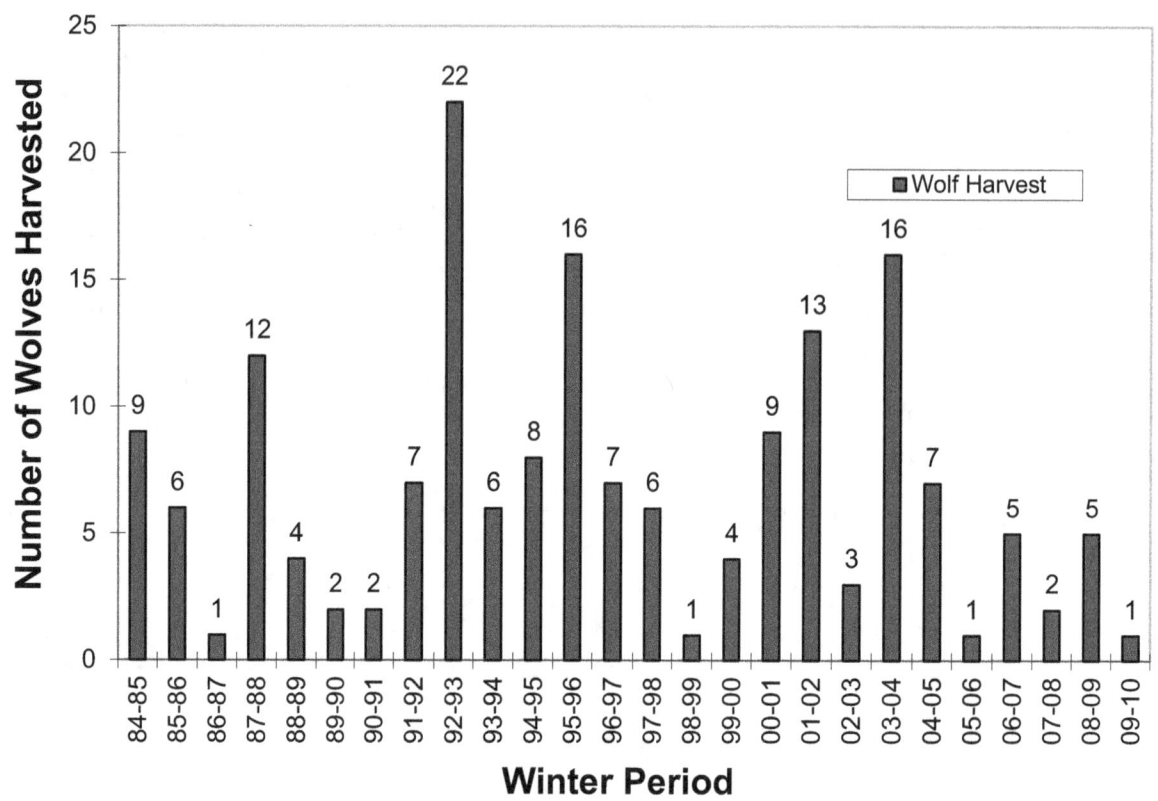

Figure 18. Harvest of wolves within and around YUCH, 1984 - 2010. From ADF&G wolf sealing records. 26 year average = 6.73.

Genetics

Blood and /or tissue samples (cheek swabs and hair roots) are collected from all captured wolves for genetic analysis from both YUCH and Denali National Park and Preserve (Denali). Unique samples were collected from over150 individual wolves from both parks. Microsatellite data taken from the DNA extracted from these samples will be analyzed to assess the baseline levels of genetic variation in each wolf population and to determine the consistency of pack lineages.

Plans for Coming Year

In November 2010 and February 2011, we plan to capture more wolves to maintain 2 or 3 collars in each pack, and search for (and hopefully catch) wolves in any new or uncollared packs using Preserve lands. During this same time frame we will also be radiotracking the collared wolves from aircraft to get accurate pack counts for fall and spring population estimates. During Spring and Fall of each biological year the wolves will be radiotracked 5 – 10 times to generate biannual population estimates and estimate pup production and survival.

Literature Cited

Burch, J. W. 2002. Ecology and demography of wolves in Yukon-Charley Rivers National Preserve, Alaska. NPS Technical Report NPS/AR/NRTR-2001/41. 72pp.

Burch, J. W. 2006. Annual report on vital signs monitoring of distribution and abundance of wolves in Yukon-Charley Rivers National Preserve. Central Alaska Network, March 2006. NPS Fairbanks.14pp.

Burch, J. W. 2007. Annual report on vital signs monitoring of distribution and abundance of wolves in Yukon-Charley Rivers National Preserve. Central Alaska Network. NPS Fairbanks. 15pp.

Burch, J. W. 2008. Annual report on vital signs monitoring of wolf (*Canis lupus*) distribution and abundance in Yukon-Charley Rivers National Preserve, Central Alaska Network: 2008 report. Natural Resource Technical Report NPS/CAKN/NRTR—2008/149. National Park Service, Fort Collins, Colorado.

Burch, J. W. 2009. Annual report on vital signs monitoring of wolf (*Canis lupus*) distribution and abundance in Yukon-Charley Rivers National Preserve, Central Alaska Network: 2009 report. Natural Resource Technical Report NPS/CAKN/NRTR—2009/228. National Park Service, Fort Collins, Colorado.

Burch, J. W., L. G. Adams, E. H. Follmann, and E. A. Rexstad. 2005. Evaluation of wolf density estimation from radiotelemetry data. Wildlife Society Bulletin 33(4):1225-1236

Fuller, T. K., L. D. Mech, and J. F. Cochrane. 2003. Wolf population dynamics. Pp. 161-191 *In* Mech, L.D., and L. Boitani, eds., Wolves: Behavior, Ecology, and Conservation. University of Chicago Press. 448 pp.

Mech L. D., L. G. Adams, T. J. Meier, J. W. Burch, B. W. Dale. 1998. The wolves of Denali. University of Minnesota Press, Minneapolis, Minnesota.

Mech, L. D., and S. M. Barber. 2002. A critique of wildlife radio-tracking and its use in National Parks. A report to the U. S. National Park Service.

Mech, L. D., and R. O. Peterson. 2003. Wolf-prey relations. Pp. 131-160 *In* Mech, L.D., and L. Boitani, eds., Wolves: Behavior, Ecology, and Conservation. University of Chicago Press. 448 pp.

Miller, B., B. Dugelby, D. Foreman, C. Martinez del Rio, R. Noss, M. Phillips, R. Reading, M. E. Soule', J. Terborgh, and L. Willcox. 2001. The importance of large carnivores to health ecosystems. Endangered species Update 18: 202-210.

National Park Service, 2001. Denali National Park and Preserve subsistence management plan. National Park Service, Denali Park, Alaska.

Ripple, W. J., and R. L. Beschta. 2003. Wolf reintroduction, predation risk, and cottonwood recovery in Yellowstone National Park. Forest Ecology and Management 184: 299-313.

Valkenburg P., D. G. Kelleyhouse, J. L. Davis, and J. M. Ver Hoef. 1994. Case history of the Fortymile caribou herd, 1920-1990. Rangifer 14: 11-22.

White, G.C. and R. A. Garrott. 1990. Analysis of wildlife radio-tracking data. Academic Press, San Diego, California.

Worton, B. J. 1989. Kernel methods for estimating the utilization distribution in home-range studies. Ecology 70:164-168.

NPS 191/108108, June 2011

www.ingramcontent.com/pod-product-compliance
Lightning Source LLC
Chambersburg PA
CBHW080348290526
45791CB00009BA/2785